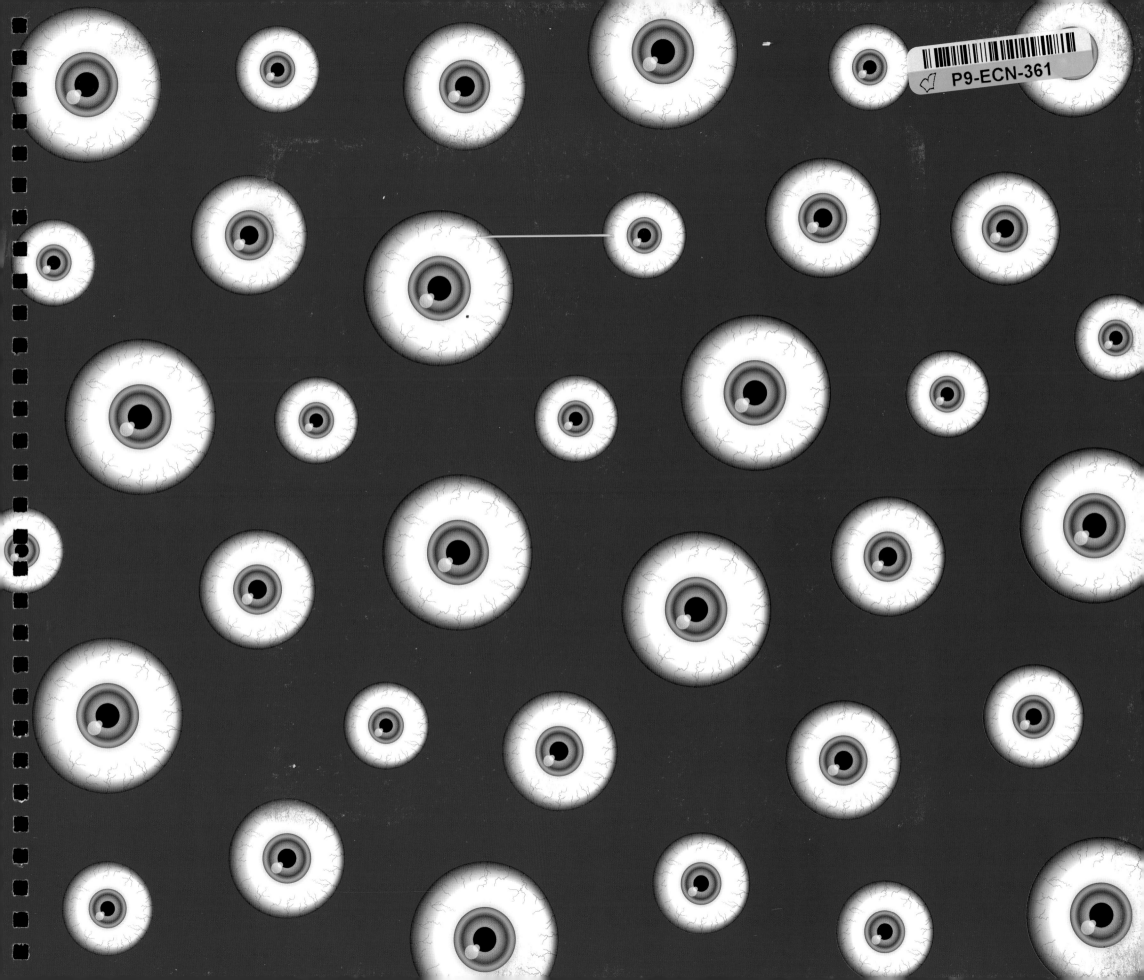

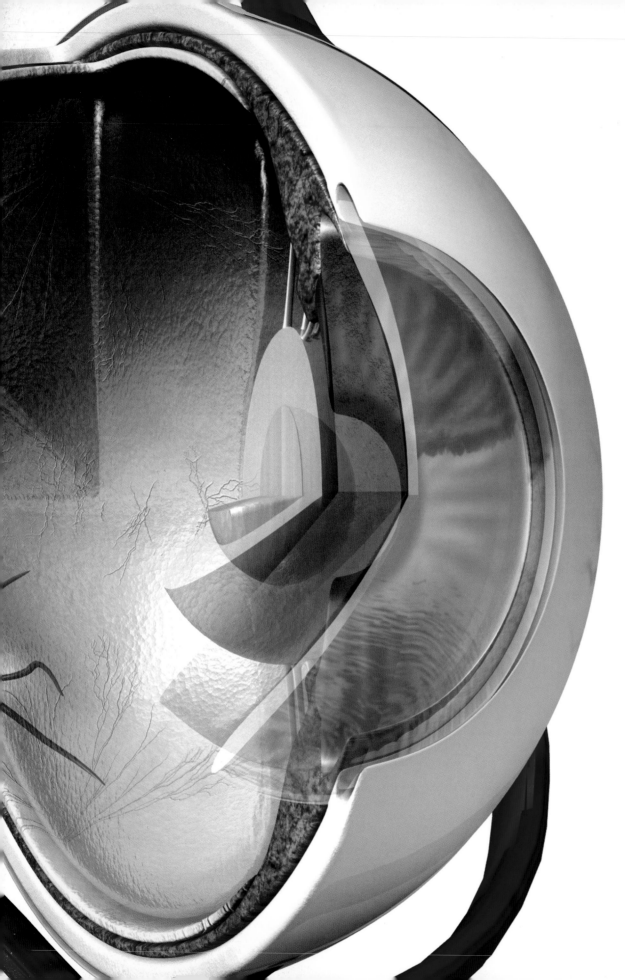

Text: Helen Otway
Illustration and design: Dynamo Design

Photography:
©shutterstock:
Gelpi, Uwe Bumann, Tatiana Popova, Yanik Chauvin, Tomasz Pietryszek, Lane V. Erickson, andrei nacu, T-Design, igor kisselev, digitalsport-photoagency, Litwin Photography, Dmitry Kosterev, Kulish Viktoriia, J. Helgason, PhotoCreate, sgame, Adrian Moisei, Indigo Fish, Tomasz Pietryszek, EcoPrint, CP Limited, Andrew Kerr, Danilo Ascione, Marko Kovacevic, Biljana Kumer, Tootles, Ruben Enger, Tihis, Galina Barskaya, Jason Stitt, Anna Dzondzua, Rachell Coe, Michael Ransburg, stanislaff, Anna Chelnokova, Aleksandr Frolov, Justina Sevostjanova, Gelpi, Maja Schon, Geoffrey Kuchera, Tijmen, Jaroslaw Grudzinski, Tischenko Irina, sima, Indigo Fish, Juriah Mosin, Zholobov Vadim, Bronwyn Photo, Pieter Pretorius, Jason Stitt, kd2, James Klotz, Chiyacat, nazira_g, George Hoffman, Stefan Redel, Jerri Adams, pnicoledolin, Nik Niklz, Martin Vrlik, Lori Skelton, Yanik Chauvin, Guy Erwood, Lisa F. Young, Dóri O'Connell, alexander s. heitkamp, Thomas Mounsey, Branislav Senic, Gleb Semenjuk, Norman Chan, Edyta Pawlowska, Aurelio, pmphoto, Brian McEntire, Vladimir Mucibabic, Victoria Alexandrova, anna karwowska, Denis Pepin, Simone van den Berg, Sz Akos, szefei, EcoPrint, Fouquin, ahnhuynh, doctor_bass, Lara Barrett, Keith A Frith, matka_Wariatka, Jhaz Photographym, electerra, Hallgerd, Stepanov, kavram, Matty Symons, Nicholas James Homrich, Alexander Abolinsh, Irina Fischer, phdpsx, Suzanne Tucker, iofoto, Donald, Stephen Coburn, Colin & Linda McKie, dwphotos, Robert A. Mansker, Robert Hardholt, Tatjana Strelkova, Dr. Morley Read, Sergey Popov V, byphoto, MaleWitch, Phillip Date, Alexander Motrenko, Sebastian Kaulitzki, Laurin Rinder, Bettina Baumgartner, Mark Bond, Terrie L. Zeller, Andrei Vorobiev, Tatiana Popova, prism_68, Tootles, Germán Ariel Berra, Suzanne Tucker, Nikita Tiunov, Shanta Giddens, Michael Pettigrew, Yu-Feng Chen, Andraž Cerar, Thomas Mounsey, Gordana Sermek, Dana E. Fry, Chris Mole, Rena Schild, Marina Cano Trueba, szisti, Leah-Anne Thompson, Dmitry Rukhlenko
©dreamstime.com:
Nicalfc, Dwart-studio, Stratum, Leloft1911
©iStockphoto.com:
dolgachov, arlindo71, Omentum, Lugo, HultonArchive, abalcazar, Jiblet
©Getty Images

TORMONT

Canadä

We acknowledge the financial support of the Government of Canada through the Book Publishing Industry Development Program (BPIDP) for our publishing activities.

Legal deposit—Bibliothèque et Archives nationales du Québec, 2008

Imported in Europe by:
Tormont Europe Ltd.
101 Furry Park Road
Dublin 5, Ireland

Printed in China

ISBN 978-2-7641-2189-4

Exploring your SENSES

Note to Parents

Discovering how the five senses work will help your child understand more about how he or she relates to the surrounding environment. There is a section in this book devoted to each sensory system and while these can be read independently of one another, it is recommended that the Smell and Taste sections be read together.

Included inside the cover of the book are activity cards relating to each section. Some of these suggest simple experiments and require food and/or equipment normally available in the home. Covering the eyes is part of some of these tests, but a blindfold should not be used on a child who does not feel comfortable with it.

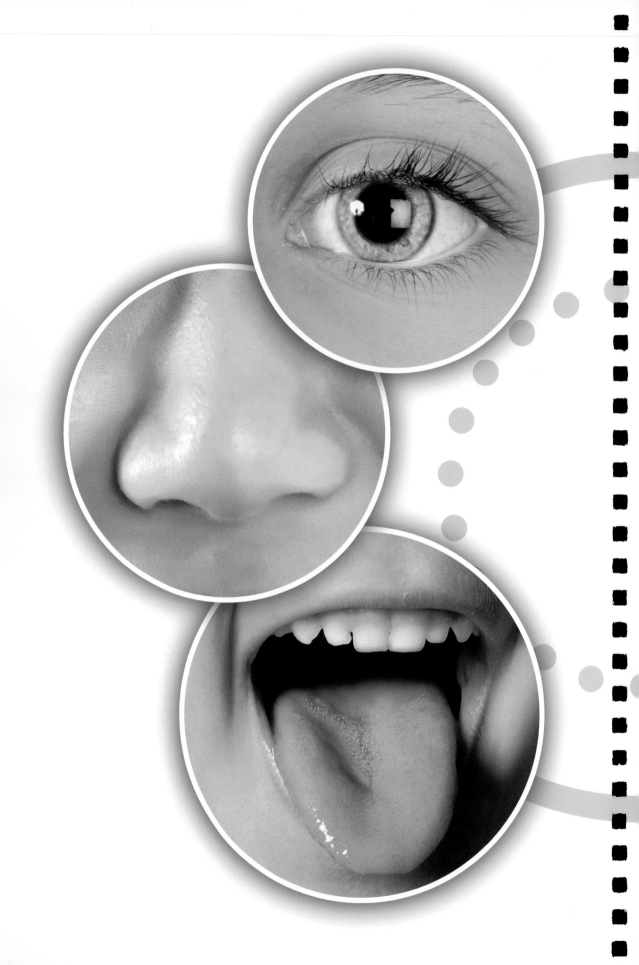

CONTENTS

 # Sight

Your eyes are amazing!

Which parts of your body let you read comics, see brilliant colors or know where to kick a ball? Which parts make tears to protect themselves and let you cry when you're sad? That's right, your eyes! From the moment you wake up, your eyes are busy collecting information about everything around you. They constantly send messages to your brain to let you know what's going on!

Sclera
The white of the eye. This is the coating of the eyeball.

Muscles
Hold the eyeball in place, and allow it to move.

Pupil
The dark hole in the middle of the iris.

Lens
Focuses light onto the retina to create an image.

Cornea
A clear dome that protects the front of the eye and focuses light into it.

Iris
The colored part of the eye that controls how much light enters it.

Retina
The light-sensitive lining at the back of the eye where the image is focused.

Optic Nerve
Takes images from the retina and sends them to the brain.

👁 Eye movement

Attached to each of your eyeballs are six ribbon-like muscles. These muscles work together to move the eye up, down, left or right and are some of the fastest-reacting muscles in your body.

BUSY MUSCLES! ❗

Your eye muscles move more than 100,000 times a day. Many of these movements happen while you're asleep and having a great dream!

👁 Around the eye

Your eyes are protected in several ways:

> The eyelashes along the edge of the eyelid keep out dirt and act a little bit like whiskers! They're an early warning system to sense if something comes too close, making the lids snap shut.

> The lids will also close automatically and scrunch up if too much light shines in.

> The eyebrows keep out dirt too, and their curved shape means that any extra moisture, such as sweat or rain, runs away from the eyes.

> The bony eye socket is a tough shield against injury.

👁 Exercise those eyes!

Your eye muscles are like any other muscles in your body: they need a little workout now and then!

To exercise them, all you need to do is:

Move your eyes straight up…then straight down. Repeat four times and take a few blinks to relax the muscles again.

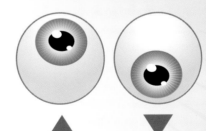

Then move your eyes to the left…and to the right. Repeat four times and blink, blink, blink!

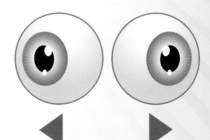

BLINKING MARVELOUS! ❗

Adults blink a lot more often than babies and children. Newborn babies blink only once or twice a minute! Use a watch to see how many times you blink in a minute.

DID YOU KNOW?

👁 *Tears are being made in your lacrimal glands all day long! The liquid gets washed across the eye each time you blink to keep those eyeballs clean and moist.*

👁 *Tear fluid is made up of water and many other chemicals. It even contains a type of oil, so that it doesn't evaporate and leave you with dry eyes!*

👁 *All animals make tears, but only humans cry when they're sad or in pain. This is when an emotion makes you produce so much tear fluid that it overflows, running down your cheeks and even down your nose!*

👁 *Newborn babies do not cry tears! Their lacrimal glands don't get going until they're a few weeks old.*

DID YOU KNOW?

- Most of the world's population has brown eyes.

- When we talk about eye color, we actually mean iris color. That means your friends with blue eyes have blue irises! The color of the iris depends on a pigment called melanin: brown eyes have much more melanin in them than blue eyes.

- Some people choose to change the color of their eyes by wearing colored contact lenses. Movie actors might use more unusual lenses if they want to get that tiger or alien look!

- Those devilish red eyes that sometimes appear on photos of your friends are from bright light reflecting off their blood-rich retinas! The flash happens too quickly for the irises to close the pupils in time.

How we see

When you look at something, the cornea focuses the light that bounces off it through the pupil. Your lens further focuses the light rays to form an upside-down image at the back of your eye and nerves take the picture message to your brain. It's your brain's job to turn the picture the right way up and make sense of what you see!

3D VISION

The brain receives a slightly different image from each eye and you need both of these to see properly. Try shutting one eye for a few minutes as you do a basic task and see how it affects your judgement!

Instant messaging

As you look around you, millions of nerve messages whizz along your optic nerve. This is a bit like a speedy internet connection from each eye to the brain, delivering masses of information to be translated into images. If the optic nerve gets damaged through illness, the connection is lost: no messages reach the brain and blindness occurs.

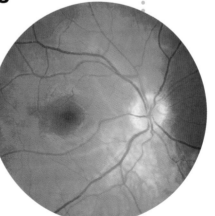

Pupil size

Your irises change the size of your pupils according to how much light there is around you.

In normal light, the iris is a kind of even, doughnut shape with the pupil as the hole!

In bright light, muscles in the iris contract to close the pupil and stop too much light getting in.

In dim light, the muscles relax to make the pupils larger and let in as much light as possible. Your pupils will also get bigger if you're scared or excited about something.

SEE FOR YOURSELF!

Sit next to a lamp with a mirror and look at your pupils. Switch the lamp on and then off again. What happens to your pupils?

The white of the eye

The tough coating of the eye is called the sclera. Although it looks completely white from a distance, it is covered with tiny pink blood vessels – look closely at a friend's sclera to check them out, but make sure you ask them first!

! EYEBALL JEWELRY

Dutch eye surgeons have taken body decoration a step too far! In 2004, they invented eyeball jewelry, in which a pretty metal shape is inserted into the sclera's sliced membrane (the conjunctiva). It's so risky that it is not legal anywhere else in the world.

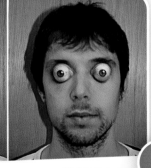

! EYE POPPING!

Some people can pop their eyes right out of their sockets. American Kim Goodman holds the world record at 0.43 inches!

A look at the lens

You have a transparent lens in each eye, sitting just behind the pupil. Its job is to bend the light rays coming into your eye so that an image is focused on the back of the eyeball. Around each lens is a ring of muscle that changes its shape depending on how close you are to what you're looking at.

When you stroke a kitten and look at its cute little nose close up, your lenses become thicker.

When you spot your friend down the street, the muscles squeeze the lenses to make them thinner.

Behind the lens

You may not know it, but you have jelly in your eyes! Its proper name is the vitreous humor and it's what gives your eyeballs their spherical shape. It is clear, so that light can shine straight through it and if it weren't there, your eyeball would collapse into a squishy mess!

DID YOU KNOW?

- The domed cornea keeps dust and germs out of your eye while it is open. To see its curved shape, look closely at your friend's eye from the side.

- It is the only part of your body that has no blood supply, as it needs to be completely transparent for you to see clearly.

- The cornea does have lots of nerve endings, though, which makes the tiniest scratch on it feel extremely painful!

- A damaged cornea can be replaced in a straightforward cornea transplant operation, but the new cornea has to come from someone who has died recently. The first successful cornea transplant was carried out in 1905.

DID YOU KNOW?

◎ *Bulls are color blind, so it's not true that red makes them angry. What gets them mad is the guy in the crazy outfit waving that cape all over the place!*

◎ *Many more men than women are color blind, around 1 in 12.*

◎ *Color blind people have to choose their jobs carefully. You wouldn't want one of them decorating your house, for example!*

◎ *A very small number of people – 0.003 % of the world's population – suffer from total color blindness. This means they see everything as if they were watching an old black and white movie!*

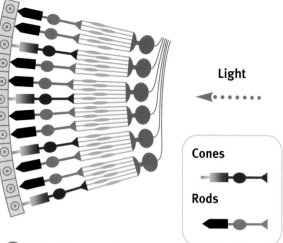

Light

Cones

Rods

◎ Seeing color

The lining at the back of the eye is called the retina and is about the size of a small postage stamp. It is filled with two sorts of light-sensitive cells:

Rods help you to see in the dark, but detect only shades of grey. They also let you see shapes and movement.

Cones work only in good light, letting you see color and details. There are three different types that respond to red, green or blue light.

You have quite a lot of these cells: more than 120 million in each eye! Whenever you have your eyes open, they're all busy sending messages to your brain about what you can see around you.

◎ Clever cones

Your cones all work together so that you can see hundreds of thousands of colors! You can see many shades of the same color too. A tomato, for example, isn't the same shade of red as a poppy. See how many shades of red you can find around your home. Then choose another color and do the same!

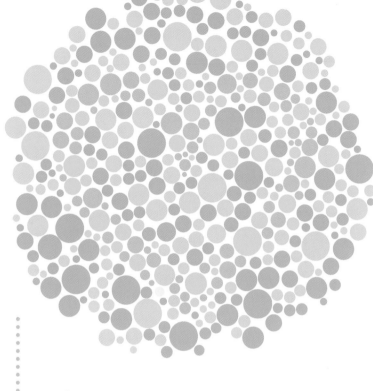

◎ Color confusion

About one person in 30 has cones that don't interpret colors in the way that they should, confusing red, green and yellow. This is called color blindness.

Look at this colorful picture. Do you see clearly what the image is? A person with color blindness will not be able to make out the image correctly, if at all.

TRY IT YOURSELF!

When you look at this picture in a good light, you should be able to see all the colors clearly. Now take it into a space with very little light where you can still make out the image. What happens to the colors?

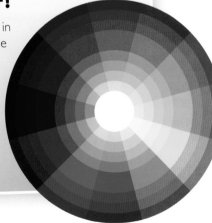

◎ Why sight goes wrong

Many people have problems with their sight, which is why it is important to get your eyes checked regularly! If someone cannot see properly, it means that his or her eyeball shape is slightly different to that of someone with perfect sight.

◎ Eyeball shape

If someone has a longer eyeball, the image will focus in front of the retina except when they are looking at things that are close to them. This is known as short sight or near sight.

Shortsighted

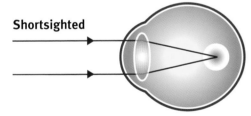

If someone has a shorter eyeball, the image will focus behind the retina and they will only be able to see things that are far away. This is known as far sight or long sight.

Eyes focus less well as a person gets older. Think of all the old people you know. How many of them wear glasses?

Farsighted

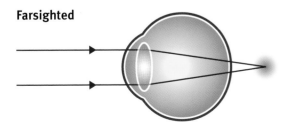

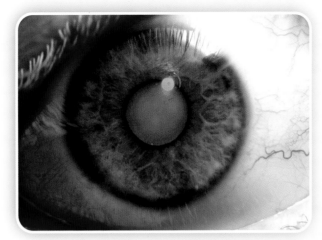

◎ Cataracts

The lens can thicken and become cloudy in old age, which means light cannot get through to the retina. This affects vision and is known as a cataract. It is very common in people over 80, who often have them in both eyes. Cataracts in young people are unusual, but can appear as a result of injury, illness or malnutrition.

◎ Eye infections

Occasionally, the eyes can become infected. Conjunctivitis is a fairly common infection that makes the eyes sore, red, itchy and a bit gunky! It is easy to clear with special drops or ointment but can affect vision if left untreated.

DID YOU KNOW?

◎ *Cataracts are the most common cause of blindness in the world. Although they are reasonably easy to treat, the operation is not available in poorer countries.*

◎ *According to the World Health Organization, 75% of the world's blindness could be prevented or treated.*

◎ *Snow blindness is the result of eyes getting sunburned from strong sunlight reflected off snow or ice. The eyes become swollen and painful, in extreme cases suffering vision loss.*

◎ *Someone who has lost an eye may suffer from phantom eye syndrome, seeing things with the missing eye and feeling pain from it.*

◎ Sight

DID YOU KNOW?

◎ OPTICAL ILLUSIONS

Images like these are known as optical illusions and are said to trick the eye. Since it is the brain that makes sense of the images, that's what is getting confused! Take a closer look and see what your brain makes of them.

ILLUSION NO. 1

Are these horizontal lines parallel to one another?

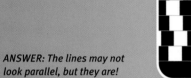

ANSWER: The lines may not look parallel, but they are!

ILLUSION NO. 2

Which is the longest horizontal line?

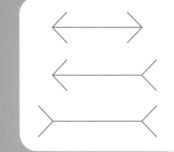

ANSWER: They are all exactly the same length!

◎ *Famous artists like Salvador Dalí and MC Escher enjoyed optical illusions and used them in some of their work.*

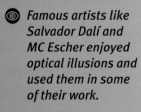

◎ Putting eyes right

People of all ages can be shortsighted or farsighted and this can be easily fixed by wearing glasses or contact lenses. An eye expert called an optician uses tests to find out what sort of lens is needed to help images focus on the retina.

◎ Eye surgery

Sight can also be corrected by laser eye surgery, where a laser is used to change the shape of the cornea. Cataracts can be removed in a simple operation that is done with a local anaesthetic, so that the patient is awake as it's being done!

◎ Eye safety

Your eyes are very precious and can never be replaced, so you should look after them! Wear sunglasses, as too much bright sunlight can damage the eyes and lead to cataracts later. You should also protect your eyes when taking part in classes or sports where they could be injured by chemicals or flying objects.

TEST YOURSELF! ❗

You should see an optician to have your eyes tested properly, but for fun you can try out the eye test in the front cover. Measure how close you need to be to see all the letters clearly. Then see how the distance compares with that of a much older person!

 Amazing animal eyes

How do our eyes compare with those of the creatures we share the planet with?

  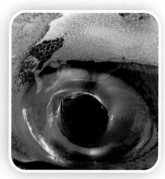 

If you've ever spotted a cat outside at night, you'll know that they have spooky glowing eyes! This glow comes from light reflecting off the special shiny surface at the back of cat's eyes that helps them to see in the dark. Look at the shape of a cat's pupils too. How are they different from yours?

Owls have huge, forward facing eyes packed with rods that are fantastic for catching prey in the dark. They cannot move their eyes, so they have to turn their heads instead. Luckily, they can do this 270° in each direction! Try being an owl and look around you by moving only your head, keeping your eyes still. How far can you see?

Someone with keen eyesight is not described as having 'eyes like a hawk' for nothing! A hawk's vision is much better than ours, as it needs to spot its prey from a distance before it can make a surprise swoop, sometimes catching a meal in midair!

The eyes of the giant squid are each about a foot wide and are among the largest in the animal kingdom! Since it lives in deep and murky waters, its eyes need to be as big as possible to make the most of what little light there is down there.

DID YOU KNOW?

. . . .

Many insects have compound eyes, which create a mosaic image from hundreds of mini eyes. Compound eyes are very sensitive to movement, which means honeybees can find flowers more easily when there's a bit of a breeze!

An ostrich's eye is bigger than its brain. Take a look next time you see one, but be sure not to get too close!

A chameleon can move and focus its eyes separately, so it misses absolutely nothing!

The most basic eyes are found in animals like snails. They do not produce images, but can tell the difference between light and dark. At least this means a snail can avoid getting sizzled in the sun!

TASTY EYEBALLS!

In some cultures, animal eyeballs are considered a delicacy. The lens and jelly are removed and replaced with a tasty filling before being cooked. Yum!!

 Expressive eyebrows

How can you tell when you're in big trouble with your mum? Or when your friend knows something you don't? It's all in the eyes! We often use our eyes and eyebrows to communicate. Look in the mirror and see how your eyes and eyebrows behave when you change your expression. Now try frowning and smiling at the same time!

Smell

Get to know your nose!

Your nose has two important jobs to do: it filters the air you breathe, making it warm and clean enough to enter your lungs, and it allows you to identify the smells around you. Many smells are pleasant, but some are just disgusting! It may not be fun smelling horrible odors, but your nose is also there to protect you: it acts as an early warning system of dangers such as fire, poisonous gases or possible infection.

Nasal cavity

The hollow space behind your nose that is lined with mucus-secreting membranes.

Cilia

Hair-like cells, even tinier than olfactory hair cells, that move back and forth to send mucus toward the throat.

Nasal hairs

Any particles that shouldn't go into the lungs, such as dust and dirt, are trapped here.

Nostril

The opening to the nasal passage that comes in all shapes and sizes!

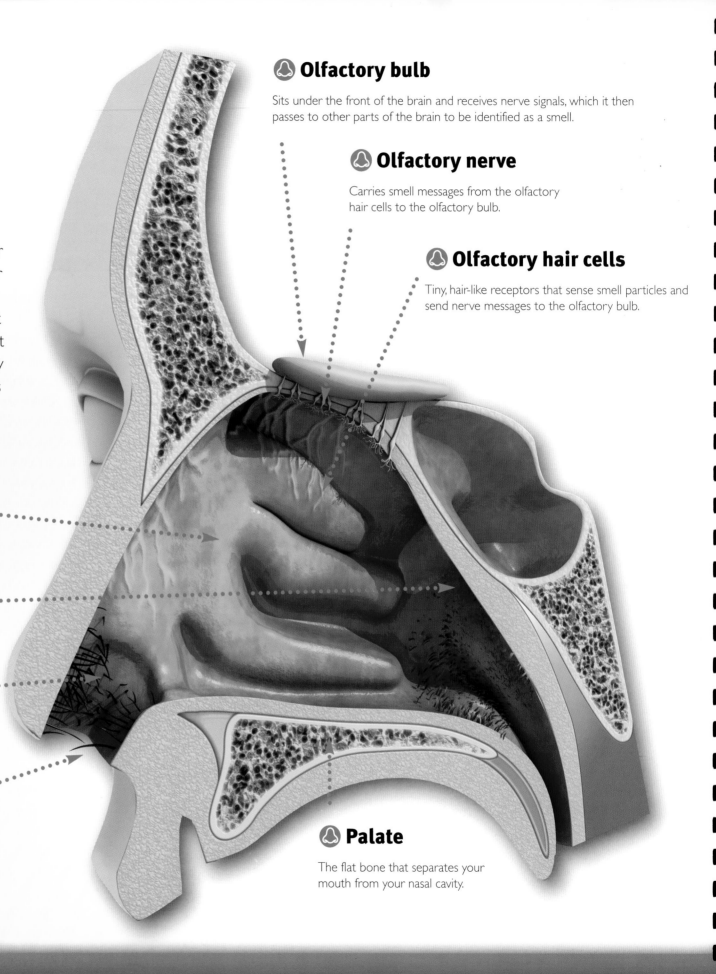

Olfactory bulb

Sits under the front of the brain and receives nerve signals, which it then passes to other parts of the brain to be identified as a smell.

Olfactory nerve

Carries smell messages from the olfactory hair cells to the olfactory bulb.

Olfactory hair cells

Tiny, hair-like receptors that sense smell particles and send nerve messages to the olfactory bulb.

Palate

The flat bone that separates your mouth from your nasal cavity.

The nose

Take a good look at your nose in a mirror! Those two holes in it are your nostrils and they're the openings to your nasal passages. Separating these passages is the septum, most of which is made of tough cartilage. You can feel it easily if you run your finger down the middle of your nose towards the tip while you give it a bit of a wiggle!

Behind the nostrils

You have a hole in your head! Your nasal cavity is the open space behind your nose. If you put your tongue on the roof of your mouth, you'll feel your palate. Right above that is your nasal cavity. It is linked to the back of the throat, which is why juice might squirt out of your nose if you laugh hard while drinking it!

DID YOU KNOW?

Take a sniff

Smells will find their way into your nose when you're just sitting around breathing normally, but a way to smell something better is by sniffing it up close! When you take a sniff, you're making the air swirl upwards to the top of your nose so that more smell particles reach the sensors on the nose's ceiling.

- *Particles trapped in the nose hairs get covered in mucus that dries out and hardens. We all know what those are called!*

- *We all have hairy noses! The hairs you can see trap all sorts of things that shouldn't go down into your lungs: dirt, dust, pollen...even little bugs!*

- *Men have more nose hair than women, especially the older guys. When those nose hairs start to dangle out of the nostrils, it's time to think about investing in a trimmer!*

- *Your nose is full of bacteria! Don't worry – most are harmless and the nasty ones are usually taken care of by your nose's trusty hair and mucus team.*

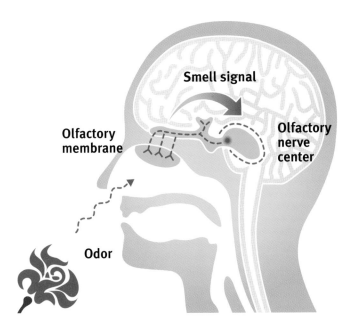

Smell signal

Olfactory membrane

Olfactory nerve center

Odor

What's that smell?

Smells are made up of tiny particles that zoom up your nose when you breathe in. Hanging from the roof of your nose are millions of hair-like receptors. When they sense an invasion of smell particles, or odor particles, they send nerve signals to the olfactory bulb under the front of the brain. This in turn sends messages to the brain and the smell is identified.

TRY IT YOURSELF

Find something that has a scent, such as a flower or a bar of soap. Hold it under your nose and breathe normally. Then sniff, sniff, sniff and smell the difference!

 # Smell

Smell and emotion

The nerves involved in smelling are linked to the part of your brain that controls emotions. This means that most smells can be classed as ones that you either like or don't like. Everyone is different, so a smell that seems great to one person can be sickening to another!

Smell and taste

We have to be able to smell our food to taste it – that's why everything seems tasteless if we have a cold. Try holding your nose as you eat something. Now let go and taste the difference! Sometimes you might actually want to taste very little, like when you have to take some yucky medicine; holding your nose will help it to go down!

DID YOU KNOW?

Lasting memories

Once your brain has identified a smell, the memory of it will stay with you for years. Think of your favorite smell. What does it remind you of? Ask your friends what their favorite smell is and see if their preferences are tied to special memories. Many people associate the smell of baking with home, or with their grandparents' home.

- 🔔 *Your nose is busy making mucus all the time! That may sound gross, but you need it to dissolve those smell particles so the brain can identify them. It also moistens the air that you breathe in before it goes down to your lungs.*

- 🔔 *So where does all that mucus go? Down your throat! In fact, you swallow about a cup of mucus each day. Okay, so that is gross!*

- 🔔 *Thousands of tiny, hair-like cilia in your nose normally sweep mucus toward your throat. These slow down when it's cold, so the mucus drips out of your nose instead!*

- 🔔 *Healthy mucus is clear and watery. When you get ill with a cold or flu, the infection makes your mucus thicken and turn yellow...or even green!*

Young noses

Your sense of smell was working well as soon as you were born, helping you to recognize your mum by her special smell. Like everything else, your sense of smell works less well as you grow older, so you have a much better sense of smell than your grandparents!

❗ SMELLS TASTY

Your sense of smell is 10,000 times more sensitive than your sense of taste! In fact, the smell of what you are eating makes up about 80% of what you taste. This means that smells from elsewhere can confuse the brain while we're eating. To see this for yourself, take a bite of something and see how it tastes. Then try eating the same thing while you hold a slice of onion or lemon under your nostrils. How does it taste now?

Nasty sniffs

While you might love a smell that your friend hates, there are some smells that everyone agrees are revolting!

 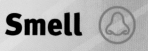

Abominable acids

Acidic smells really make your nose wrinkle! Smells that contain acid include the unmistakable stench of vomit, which can be so bad it might make you feel like vomiting. The same acid is in the smell of milk that has gone sour – it's a warning not to drink it!

When good smells go bad

A perfume that smells heavenly in its bottle might not smell so good on some people's skin. This is because perfumes are complex formulas and everyone's skin chemistry is different, so the wrong combination can create eau de moldy old cabbage!

SWEET SWEAT

Fresh sweat has no smell, as it is made mainly of water. If someone has body odor, the nasty smell is coming from the bacteria that munch on the sweat and breed in it over time. The smell is a kind of warning that the body needs a good wash!

Smelly cheese

Some of the molecules in the smell of ripe cheeses are the same as those found in rotten foods, so not wanting to eat them is a perfectly natural response. Some cheeses, such as Limburger, even contain the same bacteria that are found in body odor!

Eggy odors

Modern food storage means that you probably never smelled a bad egg…but you know what it would smell like! The rotten egg smell that is used in stink bombs is caused by hydrogen sulfide. It's present in the body, so you might also have recognized it when your friend left the room in a hurry and let you get the blame for the smell!

DID YOU KNOW?

- *The striped skunk is the smelliest mammal on Earth. It sprays a foul liquid from its anal glands, but only when threatened. So, if you see a skunk…be nice!*

- *The thorny durian fruit from Southeast Asia is said to smell of stale vomit and rotten eggs! It's so stinky that it is illegal to take it on public transport.*

- *Not all flowers smell sweet and some are really foul – the titan arum is otherwise known as the 'corpse flower' as it reeks of rotting flesh.*

- *An incredibly pungent Sardinian cheese called casu marzu contains extra protein in the form of wriggling maggots! Some fans take the maggots out before eating it…*

 # Smell

DID YOU KNOW?

- *If you gently scratch a koala, your fingers will smell of eucalyptus! This is because strong-smelling eucalyptus leaves make up a large part of its diet.*

- *Lavender smells pleasant to most people and is even said to have a calming effect, but many insects hate it! This is why dried lavender in pouches can be used to keep clothes moths away.*

- *The characteristic smell of coffee is produced by an essential oil called caffeol, released only when the coffee beans have been roasted above 392º F (200º C).*

- *The smell of freshly-cut grass is so popular that one Dutch company even trademarked the scent and used it to make its tennis balls smell grassy fresh!*

That smells nice!

A pleasant smell can really affect our mood and create a feeling of well-being, especially if it brings to mind a happy memory. Lots of research goes into products such as toiletries, air fresheners and cleaning products whose main selling point is the way they smell.

If the smell fits

Take a look at the toiletries and detergents around your home. It's likely that they will all have a fresh citrus, pine or floral smell because we associate them with cleanliness. Imagine a pizza-scented shower gel – even if you love pizza, you wouldn't want your skin to smell of it!

JUST FOR FUN

How much does your nose know? Find out by doing the smell test in the pocket on the inside of the cover!

Food aromas

The smell of cooking usually makes us feel happy, especially if we're hungry! These smell particles set off a chain reaction in the brain, preparing our mouth for food by increasing the amount of saliva in it. Once mealtimes are over, though, our reaction to food smells changes and lingering odors can become annoying!

Perfume

People have been using perfumes for thousands of years and the first ones were made from sweet-smelling herbs and spices. Plant extracts (essential oils) were first used around the 11th century, while the mixture of scented oils and alcohol that modern perfumes are based on appeared around the 14th century. There are thousands of perfumes on sale around the world today and their exact formulas are usually a secret!

Fragrance free

Lots of people find extra smells overpowering and some might even have an allergic reaction to them, so the products around your home could be fragrance free, which means they have not had any artificial smells added.

Sneezing

Sneezing is the fastest way for your body to get germs or irritating dust particles out of your nose. Some smell particles can also make people sneeze and in extreme cases can cause allergic reactions.

BETTER OUT THAN IN! !

Even a regular sneeze affects more than just your nose. Muscles throughout your body contract when you sneeze and even your heart pauses for a fraction of a second. It's a pretty explosive function and trying to stop it could be painful, so if you feel a sneeze coming, just go with it!

Hay fever

One of the most common allergies is hay fever, which is an allergy to the tree or grass pollens that are floating around at certain times of the year. If a sufferer breathes in these pollens, they become trapped in the nose and trigger a reaction that includes sneezing, watery eyes and an a scratchy throat.

Fantastic pheromones

Animals and insects produce smells called pheromones to attract a mate. Just a few of these special smell molecules from a female emperor moth can attract males from more than six miles away. People give off pheromones too, but they have to be in the same room to feel attracted to one another!

Which way?

Animal pheromones can also be used to warn of danger or give information. Ants, for example, produce a trail pheromone for the others in their colony that says, "This way for dinner, guys!" That's how lines of ants know which way to go for food!

DID YOU KNOW?

When you sneeze, the air shoots out of your nose at about 100 miles per hour. Thousands of speeding mucus droplets spray out with it too!

It's impossible to sneeze with your eyes open! It's likely that this is the body's way of stopping any ejected particles finding their way into your eyes.

The hagfish is the only kind of fish that can sneeze! It's covered in mucus and occasionally has to sneeze the slime out of its single nostril so it doesn't suffocate.

Bright sunlight can make some people sneeze. This is called photic sneezing and is inherited, so you can blame your parents if it happens to you!

 # Smell

DID YOU KNOW?

🔔 *The sense of smell can be trained to expert level. Wine tasters, for example, can name a wine just by smelling it. Some can even say in which year it was made!*

🔔 *Colds are so common because there are hundreds of different viruses that cause them. That's why there is no vaccination or cure!*

🔔 *Nasal polyps are growths in the nose that can affect someone's sense of smell. Some can grow to be as big as a grape!*

🔔 *Women generally have a better sense of smell than men. A pregnant woman is especially sensitive and certain food odors that may seem great to everyone else can make her want to throw up!*

🔔 Smelling well

All sorts of things can affect your sense of smell. Even if you're healthy, your sense of smell works less well when you first get up in the morning and gets better as the day goes on. You will also smell more when you're hungry! If you're feeling a little under the weather, your sense of smell will be affected. If you have a bad cold, all that extra mucus will make sure you cannot smell a thing!

🔔 Background smells

If you sit in your house when there's no cooking going on, what do you smell? Nothing, right? Wrong! Your house is full of smells, but because they're there all the time your brain has stopped registering them. If you have a pet dog, you don't notice their smell, whereas a visiting friend who has no pets will be able to smell it as soon as he or she walks into the hallway.

🔔 Odorless dangers

Although most nasty substances have a bad smell that warns us of danger, there are dangerous fumes that have no smell. Carbon monoxide, for example, comes from some forms of burning and is given out by car engines. Some central heating furnaces also produce these fumes that can be deadly if they stay inside the home, so it's important for them to be checked regularly and to have a carbon monoxide detector nearby.

🔔 When smell goes wrong

Some people cannot smell at all. As with deafness or blindness, this can be a problem from birth or can be caused by illness or injury. Although loss of smell doesn't affect everyday life as much as loss of sight or hearing might, it does change the quality of life in a big way. Imagine how dull it would be if you could smell nothing and taste very little!

TRY IT YOURSELF !

Ask a friend what they can smell when they come into your home. The next time you visit them, see how many smells you can pick up that are not in your house!

🐾 Super sniffers

You can sense thousands of smells, but these animals can do even better!

🐾 Bloodhound

Dogs sniff around so much because they have an excellent sense of smell. Bloodhounds have been specially bred to track people and have a sense of smell that is thousands of times better than yours – a bloodhound looking for you would sense your smell in a room hours or even days after you had left it!

🐾 Polar bear

The bloodhound may be a champion sniffer, but the land mammal with the most sensitive nose is the polar bear. It can smell a seal from 18 miles (29 km) away and will actively hunt a human for food if it picks up his or her scent! Polar bears also have special nostrils that close when they go underwater.

DID YOU KNOW?

🐾 *Dolphins have no nose and just one nostril...at the top of their head! This means they have no sense of smell but can taste things and do have favorite fish dinners.*

🐾 *The star-nosed mole looks like its nose just exploded! It uses its 22 nose tentacles to detect and eat prey in less than a second.*

🐾 *The proboscis monkey from Borneo has the longest nose of any primate! The nose dangles over the monkey's mouth and helps it to make its characteristic honking sound.*

🐾 *The kiwi is the only bird to have nostrils at the end of its bill. This means it can stick its bill in the ground and sniff out tasty worms and insects!*

🐾 Shark

Sharks have the most highly developed sense of smell of all fish and are fierce predators. They can smell prey from great distances and are able to detect one part of blood in 100 million parts of water. Some are not picky about what kind of blood it is, which is why a human seems like a tasty snack!

🐾 Elephant

As you would expect, an elephant has a great sense of smell, too. The trunk is a combined upper lip and long nose made up of thousands of muscles. It's sensitive enough to pick up a blade of grass, but strong enough to break a tree branch. An elephant will hold its trunk up and twist it back and forth to have a good sniff around for nearby friends or food!

 # Taste

Take a look at the tongue!

Your tongue may look totally different from your nose, but it works in a similar way by sending nerve signals to the part of your brain that identifies flavors in food and drink. The brain adds this information to the smell signals it's receiving at the same time and works out what's in your mouth. Your sense of taste also works with your sense of smell to warn you that something is not safe to eat: rotten food and poisonous plants generally taste so disgusting that you will spit them out!

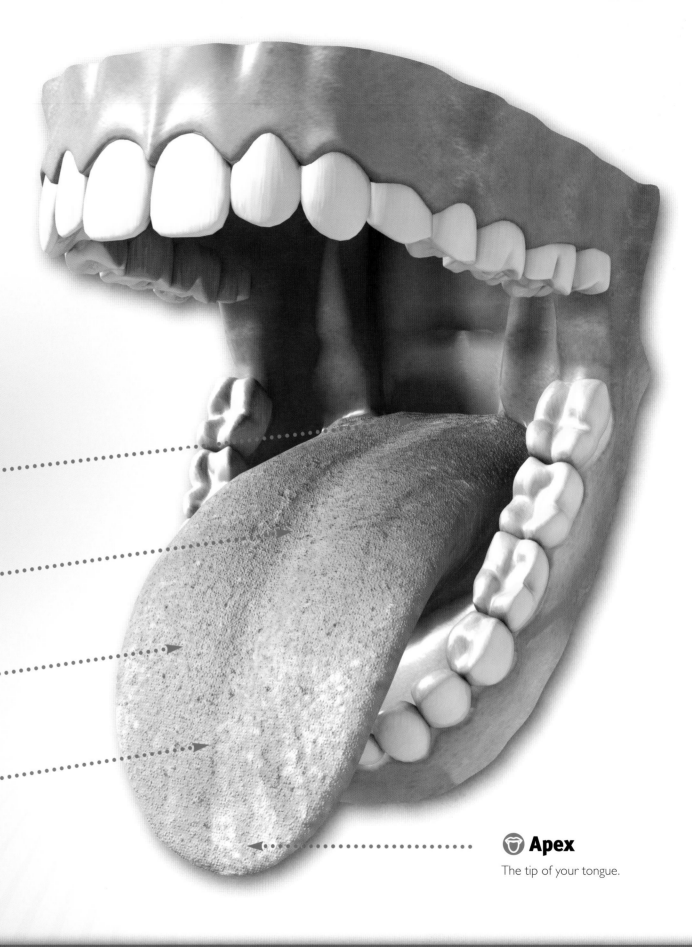

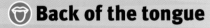 Back of the tongue
The area with the largest papillae.

Center of the tongue
The area with the fewest papillae.

Epithelium
The tongue's surface.

Papillae
The pimples you can see that contain your taste buds.

Apex
The tip of your tongue.

22

 ## Pimply papillae

Stick out your tongue and look at it closely in the mirror. (You might want to make sure there's no one else around first!) All those lumps and bumps are called papillae. They give the tongue a rough surface to grip food with and they're lined with taste receptors called taste buds.

SEE FOR YOURSELF

Take a small amount of blue or green food coloring and use a cotton swab to put some on the end of your tongue. Look in the mirror again to see how all those little papillae show up!

Taste

DID YOU KNOW?

....

- *Your taste buds die after about a week! Don't worry – they don't all die at the same time and the ones that do are quickly replaced with new ones.*

- *As you get older, though, the dead taste buds don't get renewed. An older person may have only 5,000 – that's half the number that you have – so their sense of taste is not as good.*

- *The way your papillae are laid out is different from anyone else in the world! Your tongue print is unique to you, just as your fingerprints are.*

- *You have more than 2,000 taste buds that aren't on your tongue! They're dotted around your throat and the roof of your mouth.*

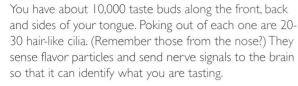

 ## Saliva

Saliva is what keeps your mouth moist and extra is produced when you eat to help you chew your food. It also works in much the same way as the mucus in your nose by dissolving flavor particles so that the cilia can detect them. If you had no saliva, you wouldn't be able to taste anything at all!

SPIT SOUP!

One type of swift makes its whole nest from saliva strands! These nests are highly prized in parts of Asia and are cooked to make goopy bird's nest soup.

 ## Taste buddies

You have about 10,000 taste buds along the front, back and sides of your tongue. Poking out of each one are 20-30 hair-like cilia. (Remember those from the nose?) They sense flavor particles and send nerve signals to the brain so that it can identify what you are tasting.

 # Taste

Basic tastes

You can recognize lots of different flavors, but the five main tastes that can be detected by your taste buds are sweet, sour, bitter, salty and the recently identified savory, also known as umami. Everything you eat is made up of one or more of these flavors.

TINGLY TONGUE

If you eat something hot and spicy, you get a tingle on your tongue! That funny feeling comes from your pain receptors, which normally sense heat and are stimulated by the chemicals in foods such as chili peppers.

TONGUE MAP

It used to be thought that each of these flavors was sensed by certain parts of the tongue, but modern research has shown that most areas of the tongue sense all of these flavors. Each taste bud senses only one taste, but you have a mixture of taste buds all over your tongue.

Muffins taste SWEET

Chips taste SALTY

The center of the tongue

You have very few, if any, taste buds in the center of your tongue. See for yourself by doing the taste test in the pocket on the inside of the cover!

Lime juice tastes SOUR

Cheese tastes SAVORY

Coffee tastes BITTER

Super strong muscles

Try keeping your tongue still – it's difficult to do for long. Even if you're not using it to eat or talk, your tongue is busy making you swallow saliva when you're sitting around reading this or even while you're sleeping!

Your tongue is made up of many groups of muscles that work in different ways, depending on what you're using it for. You might be licking your lips, talking, swallowing, moving food around your mouth or just concentrating really hard on your homework!

Talk the talk

The tongue is essential for speech, as it is involved in making most vowel and consonant sounds. To make a 't' sound, the tip of your tongue touches the front of the roof of your mouth. The back of the tongue touches the back of your palate to make a 'g' sound. Try paying attention to what your tongue is doing while you say your name!

TONGUE TWISTERS

Your tongue can move in all sorts of ways, but some phrases are just too much for it! Try saying 'she sells sea shells' over and over again. Then see how many times you can say 'Irish wristwatch' before your tongue gives up on you!

BRRRRRR buds!

Your tongue's muscles slow down if they're cold and your taste buds won't work as well either. Take a bite of something and see how it tastes. Suck on an ice cube for 30 seconds and then take another bite of the same thing. How does it taste now?

BURNT buds!

Be careful not to eat or drink anything that is too hot. If you burn your taste buds, they will feel numb for a few days and won't work properly!

DID YOU KNOW?

- 85% of people can curl their tongue into a tube. Give it a try and see if you're in the majority too!

- Black hairy tongue is a black, green or brown fungal infection that causes swollen taste buds and makes the tongue look furry!

- Strawberry tongue is another infection, which makes the papillae swell up so that the tongue looks like a plump strawberry.

- Smoking is bad for the taste buds as it reduces their sensitivity. In fact, smoking is just bad for the whole body!

Taste

DID YOU KNOW?

- *Although poisonous foods usually have a bitter flavor, highly toxic death cap mushrooms apparently taste delicious! That's why you should never pick your own mushrooms unless an expert has told you it is safe.*

- *Some people can have 20,000 taste buds – that's double tasting power! These 'supertasters' are more likely to be women than men.*

- *The weirdest ice cream flavors are found in Japan. Among others, you can choose from raw horsemeat, eel, cactus, crab or octopus!*

- *You should be glad you're not a cat – they don't taste anything sweet at all!*

Tongue TLC

It's easy to take your tongue for granted, but you need to look after it! Give it a quick brush when you clean your teeth and visit the dentist regularly to keep that tongue in tip-top condition.

THINGS THAT MAKE YOU GO OUCH! ❗

Sometimes you might get an ulcer on your tongue, from either biting it accidentally or having a minor infection. Although these are very painful, especially if you eat anything sour, they usually heal after a few days.

Eat well

You've just learned that your tongue is specially designed to sense all the tastes in a balanced diet, so do it a favor and use it to the max! Eat plenty of vegetables, some carbohydrates (such as pasta or rice), a little protein (such as meat or cheese) and satisfy any sweet cravings with the natural sugars in fruit. Okay, one or two other sweet treats won't do you any harm once in a while!

Tasty jobs

Some people use their sense of taste in their jobs. Chefs always taste what they're cooking, which means pastry chefs trying desserts all day can end up with tooth decay if they don't take care of their choppers! For an expert wine taster, one sip is enough to tell which grapes were used in making the wine and what vintage it is.

👅 Top tasters

If you think your tongue looks funny, take a look at some of these!

👅 Giraffe

Giraffes have blue-black tongues that can be 20 inches (50 cm) long! The dark color stops them getting sunburnt, as those tongues are busy stretching for acacia leaves most of the day. As acacia trees are thorny, giraffes also have thick, sticky saliva to coat any thorns that might get into the mouth.

👅 Butterfly

Your mom would probably be pretty cross if you stuck your feet in your lunch to taste it! Butterflies can do just that: when looking for a place to lay eggs, they stand on a leaf to taste whether their little caterpillars will be able to munch on it when they hatch.

👅 Snake

Many reptiles use the tip of their tongue to smell. A snake sticks out its tongue to collect any smell particles and whips them into the mouth to be identified. The fork in the tongue helps the snake to tell which direction the smell is coming from, so it knows which way to go for dinner!

👅 Chameleon

Chameleons are fairly slow-moving, so they have long, sticky tongues to catch their prey with instead! When they spot a tasty snack nearby, they unfurl their tongue at high speed. The ball of muscle on the tip acts as a suction cup to trap the insect so it can be drawn into the mouth for chomping.

HORNY TONGUE! ❗

Snails have tongues that are covered with horny teeth, which they scrape over the vegetation they're feeding on.

DID YOU KNOW?

· ·

- 👅 *The biggest tongue on the planet belongs to the blue whale and is the size of an elephant – that's three tons of tongue!*

- 👅 *The woodpecker has a secret weapon: a tongue that is as long as its body and has a barb on the end for skewering grubs!*

- 👅 *Blood-sucking parasite cymothoa exigua latches on to a tongue and shrivels it up, then replaces it with its own body! Your tongue is safe, though – it's only interested in fishy ones.*

- 👅 *A giant anteater uses its sticky tongue to snap up around 30,000 ants and termites in one day!*

Hearing

Hearing things

Your ears let you hear everything from a friend's whisper to a rumble of thunder. You think of ears as those funny-shaped things at each side of a person's head, but these are nothing more than skin and cartilage and all they do is direct sound waves into the opening of the ear canal. The tiny parts that sense these waves and make you hear them as sounds are right inside your head and also help you to keep your balance.

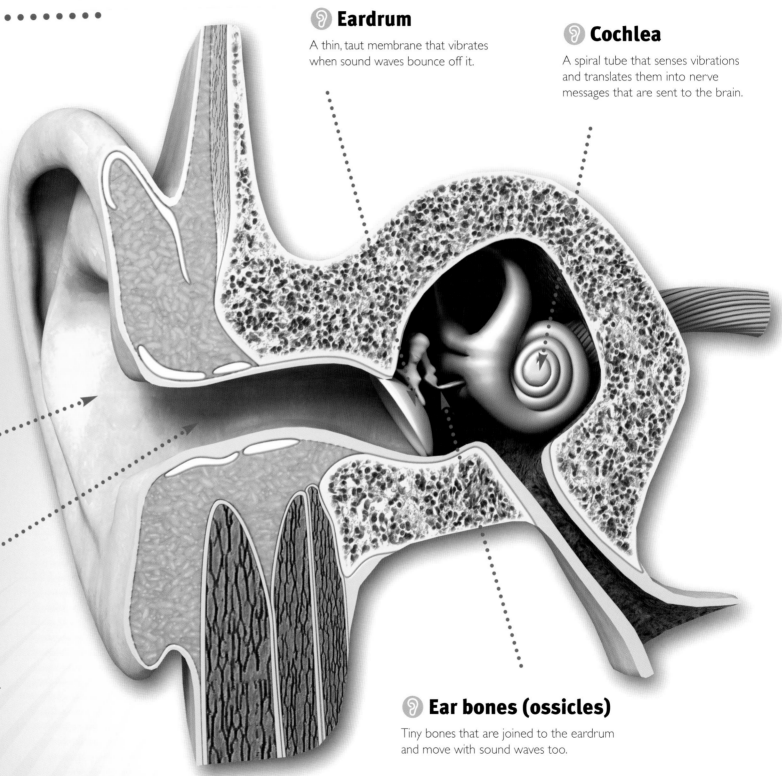

Eardrum
A thin, taut membrane that vibrates when sound waves bounce off it.

Cochlea
A spiral tube that senses vibrations and translates them into nerve messages that are sent to the brain.

Ear flap
The part of the ear that you can see.

Ear canal
The tube that leads from the outside world to your eardrum.

Ear bones (ossicles)
Tiny bones that are joined to the eardrum and move with sound waves too.

Ear sections

Your hearing system is made up of three sections: the outer ear, the middle ear and the inner ear. They all work together to let you hear the sounds around you.

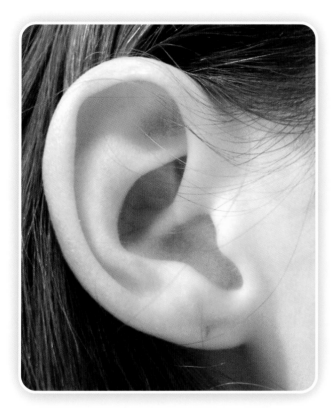

The outer ear

The outer ear is made up of the ear flap that you can see and the ear canal that leads down to the eardrum. The ear flap's shape helps to funnel sound waves into the ear canal and also protects the opening from dust, dirt, bugs or anything else that might float in. Some people like to decorate theirs with an earring or two!

WONDERFUL WAX

Down in your ear canals, lots of glands are busy making earwax! You might think that gooey stuff is gross, but it does a great job of protecting the ear by keeping away dirt and bacteria that might cause an infection.

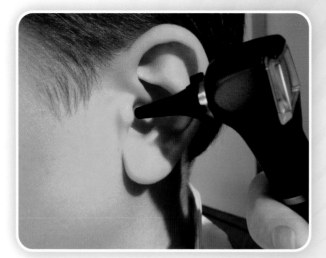

A view of the canal

If you have a sore ear, a doctor will use a special instrument to take a look inside and find out what's wrong. By shining a light into the ear canal, the doctor will be able to see all the way down to your eardrum!

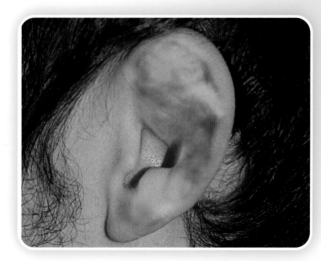

Cauliflower ear

You might have noticed that some athletes, such as football players or boxers, have even funnier-looking ears than the rest of us! An ear that has lumps and bumps in all the wrong places is called a cauliflower ear and is caused by knocks so hard that they damage the skin and cartilage for good.

DID YOU KNOW?

- *Your ears grow all through your life, but unfortunately they don't make you hear any better! They grow really slowly, too, so don't worry about your grandchildren calling you Dumbo.*

- *Earwax can be yellow, orange, grey or brown and can be gooey or crumbly! The drier stuff comes loose and falls out when you talk, chew or swallow.*

- *Otitis is an infection of the ear canal that makes the ear feel sore and itchy. It can also make the ear produce a nasty-smelling discharge!*

- *Indian man Radhakant Bajpai has hairs sprouting from his ears that measure a record-breaking 5.19 inches long!*

Hearing

The middle ear

At the end of the ear canal are the eardrum and three tiny ear bones, making up what's known as the middle ear. Each of the three bones is named for its distinctive shape: the hammer, the anvil and the stirrup. They were named in a time when there were a lot more blacksmiths around than there are now!

The inner ear

The inner ear is made up of three loops called semicircular canals and the snail shell-shaped cochlea. These parts are all filled with fluid and help your balance as well as your hearing.

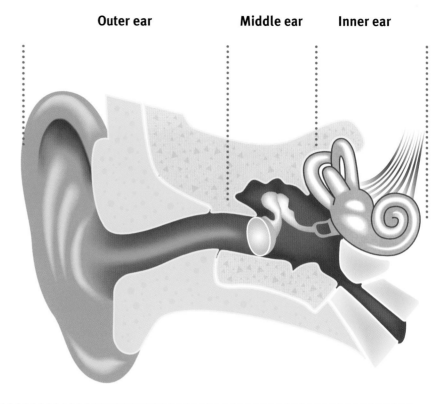

Outer ear   Middle ear   Inner ear

DID YOU KNOW?

- *An eardrum that has been damaged can have a hole in it, which is known as a perforated eardrum and reduces the sense of hearing. The eardrum is made of skin, remember, so it does eventually heal and the hearing gets back to normal.*

- *Being struck by lightning can give you perforated eardrums! It can also leave you with burns, cataracts and paralysis, so if there's an electric storm going on...stay inside.*

- *The stirrup is the smallest bone in your body!*

- *You have a tube that leads from your middle ear to your throat. It's called the Eustachian tube and is normally closed. It opens with a pop when there's a change in air pressure – that's what you hear when you're taking off or landing in an airplane!*

How we hear

When something makes a sound, it makes the surrounding air move. These sound waves travel down the ear canal and bounce off the eardrum, making it vibrate. As it's attached to the ear bones, the vibrations wobble the hammer, then the anvil and finally the stirrup. These movements make waves in the cochlear fluid that are converted into nerve signals to the brain. The brain then works out what sound you are hearing.

! NERVE SIGNALS

The nerve signals are sent from inside your cochlea by tiny, hair-like cells – yes, those again! There are thousands of them and if they sense the tiniest movement in the cochlear fluid, they let the brain know in an instant.

See for yourself

The eardrum is a very thin piece of skin that is stretched tight, just like on a drum you might use in music class. To see how it works, place a few grains of uncooked rice on a drum if you have one; if not, you can pull some plastic wrap tight over a bowl and use that instead. Whack a baking tray or something equally noisy close to your drum and you will see the rice grains jump slightly. The sound waves from the bang make the skin vibrate, just as your eardrum does!

🦻 The sound of silence

There are very few places in the world where you can find yourself in total silence! Just as you are surrounded by a whole host of smells, there are many sounds nearby that you often don't notice. Focus on the sounds around you right now. How many can you hear?

🦻 Sounds like an echo

In open spaces, sound waves can bounce off surfaces and the sound can be heard a second time, or even several times, when it comes back! This is called an echo. Mountainous areas are ideal for trying out echoes, but you can get echo effects in large indoor spaces too.

❗ SOUND LEVELS

The loudness of a sound is measured in decibels. Your friend's whisper is around 20 decibels, while an airplane engine close by is over 150 decibels. Any sounds over the level of 95 decibels can hurt your ears and a sound over 130 decibels can cause deafness.

🦻 Stereo sound

Having two ears means that your brain receives two lots of information about what you are hearing. Not only do you hear the sound, but you also know where it's coming from and whether what's making the sound is moving. Find out more by doing the hearing test in the pocket on the inside of the cover!

🦻 Sounds good

Sounds greatly affect our mood: the gentle lapping of ocean waves can make us feel relaxed, while the screech of fingernails down a blackboard can make us want to scream! Music is a sound that can bring out many different emotions and our whole bodies respond automatically to its rhythm.

DID YOU KNOW?

🦻 *If an aircraft zooms along faster than the speed of sound, it will create a sonic boom. This sounds like an explosion and is over 200 decibels!*

🦻 *Sound waves can be used to create pictures of what's going on inside your body! The waves in an ultrasound scan travel freely though fluid but bounce off any solid body parts, forming an image on a screen for examination.*

🦻 *The cicada is one noisy insect! It vibrates membranes on its abdomen to make a sound that can be as loud as 100 decibels. Only the males can do this – the females just have to put up with the racket!*

🦻 *The blue whale makes the loudest sound of any living being. Its 'singing' can reach levels of over 180 decibels and can be heard more than 500 miles (800 km) away!*

Hearing

DID YOU KNOW?

- *Noise pollution is a problem all over the world, with the biggest contributor being motor vehicles. Some car companies are working hard to make ever quieter engines!*

- *Constant noise is bad for your health and can lead to stress, anxiety and feelings of aggression.*

- *Ear mites are tiny white bugs that live in the ear canal and munch on tasty earwax. Don't panic, they're found only in animal ears!*

- *Lots of children have glue ear. The middle ear is normally air-filled so that the ear bones can move freely, but it can fill with a sticky fluid that gums everything up and dulls hearing. It's usually painless and clears by itself.*

Ear damage

Injury, illness, noise and water can all affect your sense of hearing temporarily, but if the tiny, hair-like cells in the cochlea are damaged, this can lead to problems for life.

Safe sounds

People who work in noisy environments wear special ear covering to protect their inner ears from damage. You need to look after your ears, too! Even if you like loud music, be careful and keep the sound levels reasonable, especially if you're using headphones. If you don't, you won't be able to hear any music at all in a few years' time!

Water in the ears

Our ears are not really designed to have water in them, as it washes away that all-important earwax! If the ear is flooded occasionally, the water will usually drain out without any problems. It might take a few hours, as you've probably found out after going swimming. If the water doesn't drain out, though, it can lead to an infection. If you go swimming a lot or tend to have ear problems, use some earplugs whenever you go into the water.

Don't go in ear!

Any doctor will tell you that you should never stick anything smaller than your elbow in your ear. Poking your finger inside will introduce germs or do some damage and cleaning it with a cotton swab can push wax down the ear canal, causing a blockage. If you bathe or shower regularly, there's no need to do anything else to your ears!

Which way out?

Although it doesn't happen very often, you might find that you have an uninvited guest in your ear! Insects that find their way down your ear canal are just lost and trying to find their way out again. The only trouble is that all the noise a bug makes is amplified and it sounds like a killer monster insect from a movie! If it ever happens to you, the best thing to do is to keep calm and wait for the bug to make an exit. If it doesn't come out, let a grown-up call your doctor for advice.

IT'S A MYTH!

There is no way that an earwig, or any other bug for that matter, can eat its way through your brain from one ear to the other. Don't let anyone tell you otherwise!

Hearing problems

Think about how many times you have used your sense of hearing today and especially how you have used it during communication. You might have had a conversation with your dad at home or chatted with your friend on the telephone; life would be very different if you had no sense of hearing at all.

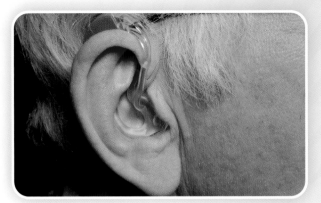

Failing ears

Your sense of hearing will fail with old age, but this can be helped with a hearing aid. It works by picking up sound waves and converting them into electrical signals that are then played back into the ear as a louder sound.

Another way of communicating

Someone who is born deaf cannot hear their own voice or anyone else's. They still have the same thoughts and feelings, so they communicate these by using their hands, bodies and facial expressions in sign language.

A MANUAL ALPHABET

Aa Bb Cc Dd Ee Ff Gg

Hh Ii Jj Kk Ll Mm

Nn Oo Pp Qq Rr Ss

Tt Uu Vv Ww Xx Yy Zz

This is the alphabet for American Sign Language.

HEAR IT YOURSELF

If you put your hands over your ears, you can hear a whooshing sound. This is caused by sound waves bouncing off your hands, ears and eardrum. The whooshing sound of tinnitus is much louder and doesn't go when you take your hands away!

All in the head

If you hear a sound that annoys you, all you have to do is switch it off or move away. Imagine, though, if you had to live with an irritating noise inside your head 24/7! Someone who has tinnitus can hear buzzing, ringing, whistling or hissing in one or both ears all the time. There are several possible causes, such as injury or earwax buildup, and usually it doesn't last long.

DID YOU KNOW?

- *Great German composer Ludwig van Beethoven began to suffer from bad tinnitus and hearing loss in his twenties. He continued to compose and perform masterpieces, even when he was completely deaf.*

- *American inventor Thomas Edison lost most of his hearing at a young age as a result of many childhood ear infections. It didn't affect his inventing skills, though!*

- *Loss of hearing in old age could be due to a lifetime of noise. A study of African tribesmen who had never been exposed to transport noise showed that the older men could hear just as well as the younger ones!*

- *Some tinnitus can be heard by other people! In one form of the condition, muscle spasms can make clicking or crackling sounds that are audible to anyone listening close by.*

Hearing

- *Weightlessness can be achieved by zooming up and down in an airplane, causing the mother of all motion sickness in its passengers. These airplanes are used for training astronauts and have been nicknamed 'Vomit Comets'!*

- *Some people can feel seasick for months after being on a boat. Sufferers of mal de débarquement or disembarkation syndrome feel a swaying sensation and sickness, long after getting back to land. Thankfully, it is a very rare condition!*

- *Some ear infections can make you throw up! A virus that affects the inner ear can upset your balance and make you feel as if you have motion sickness.*

- *Dutchman Niek Vermeulen has spent the last three decades collecting airline sick bags and now has more than 5,000. Let's hope they're all empty!*

Ears and balance

The tiny, hair-like cells inside the fluid-filled parts of the inner ear sense movement as well as sounds. The brain uses this information along with messages from the eyes to tell which way is up!

Feeling dizzy

If you spin round and round on the spot or on some playground equipment, you feel dizzy for a few moments afterwards. The liquid in your inner ear carries on spinning after you have stopped and this is sensed as movement, so you get that funny feeling!

Space sickness

If the brain gets confused while you're in a car or a plane, imagine what would happen if you went into space! The lack of gravity there means the nerve signals become even more difficult for the brain to make sense of, causing headaches, nausea, loss of balance and feelings of confusion.

> **!**
> ## SEE FOR YOURSELF
> Half fill a jar with water and swirl it round a few times. Place the jar down and see how the water carries on moving, even though the jar is still. That's what happens to the fluid in your ear!

Motion sickness

When traveling, especially in a boat, the brain sometimes has trouble making sense of all the messages about movement coming from the ears, eyes and body. This can lead to dizziness and vomiting, but the good news is that these days we can take pills to stop it!

Brilliant balance

Your sense of balance can be trained to expert level. After plenty of practice, people who take part in activities such as gymnastics or yoga can make tricky balancing poses look incredibly easy!

 All ears

You've just learned how good your ears and balance are. See how they compare with those of other animals!

African elephant

The African elephant has the largest ears of any animal! They work well for hearing, allowing elephants to communicate with each other over long distances, and also act as an effective air-conditioning system – when the elephant gets too hot, it flaps its ears around to cool off.

DID YOU KNOW?

- *Cats have an amazing sense of balance. Their extra-sensitive inner ears work with the tail to let them walk along a narrow fence or get comfy for a nice rest on the top of an open door!*

- *Dogs can hear sounds that we cannot. If you see someone blow into a dog whistle, you might think there's nothing happening, but their dog will soon come running!*

- *Mice can squeak so that we can't hear them! They can sense very high frequency sounds and use them to communicate so that any nearby predatory animal won't be aware of them.*

- *A giraffe can clean its own ears...with its tongue! We told you it was long!*

Horse

Many mammals can twist their ears back and forth to hear a sound better. It's a shame we can't do that! A horse can move its ears around by 180° to pick up the direction of a sound and has very sharp hearing. It also has a highly developed sense of balance – quite handy if there's a person on its back!

Bat

Bats find their way around in the dark by using their own sonar system. They let out high-pitched squeaks and can hear how their sounds echo off objects nearby. This is called echolocation and gives the bat an accurate picture of everything around it, including something nice for dinner!

Dolphin

What the dolphin lacks in smell, it makes up for in hearing! It has a far keener sense of hearing than we do, using its jaw as well as its ears to pick up vibrations underwater. Dolphins also use echolocation to track down prey from a distance, sending out clicking sounds and sensing how the sound waves come back.

Touch

Sensitive skin

If you closed your eyes and held out your hands to feel a mystery object, could you tell the difference between a cat and a crocodile? Of course you could! Your sense of touch comes from millions of nerve endings in your skin that give you information about how things feel. These sensors are also constantly sending messages to the brain about your body, such as whether you're feeling hot, cold, in pain or uncomfortable.

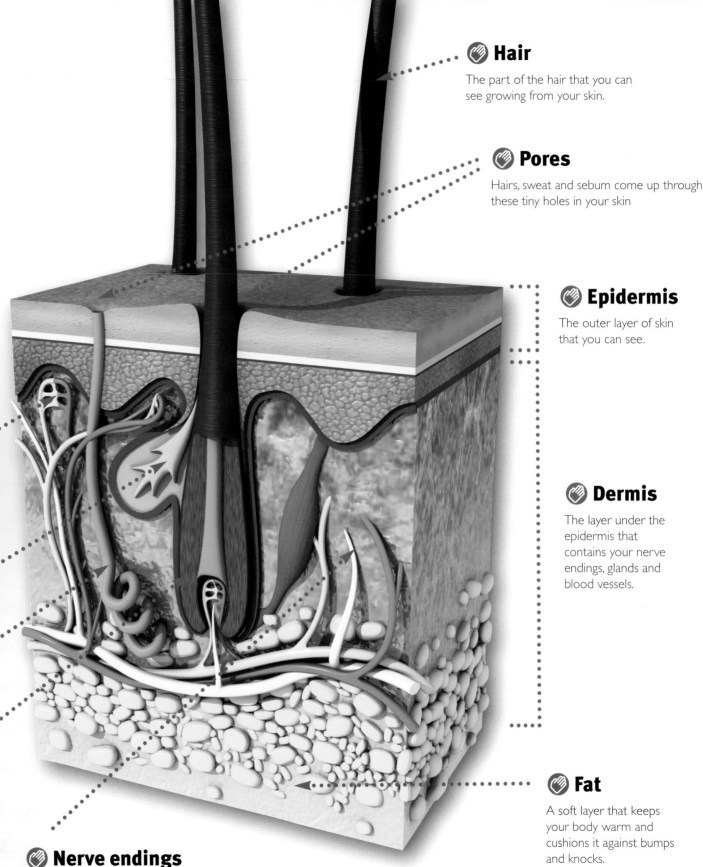

Capillaries
Tiny blood vessels that bring oxygen-rich blood to the skin cells and carry away waste.

Sebaceous gland
Glands that produce oils to help keep your hair and skin from drying out.

Sweat gland
Glands that produce the moist sweat you need to keep cool.

Hair follicle
The part rooted in the fat layer where the hair grows from.

Nerve endings
Sensors that send nerve messages to the brain about what you are touching.

Hair
The part of the hair that you can see growing from your skin.

Pores
Hairs, sweat and sebum come up through these tiny holes in your skin

Epidermis
The outer layer of skin that you can see.

Dermis
The layer under the epidermis that contains your nerve endings, glands and blood vessels.

Fat
A soft layer that keeps your body warm and cushions it against bumps and knocks.

The skin you're in

You might not think of your skin as an organ, but that's what it is. In fact, if you could step out of it and weigh it before laying it out on the floor, you'd find out that it's your heaviest and biggest organ! It's just as important as your other organs, too. Apart from giving you your sense of touch, it protects you from dirt and germs, keeps you at the right temperature and holds your insides inside!

DID YOU KNOW?

What you see

The outer layer of skin that you can see is part of the epidermis and it's dead! New cells are constantly moving up from the base of the epidermis to the surface, where they dry up and die. The good thing about this layer is that it's waterproof, so nothing leaks out and you don't soak up water while you're in the bath!

Hairy skin

If you look at your skin, you'll see there are lots of hairs growing from it. Although the part you can see is dead too, the hairs are sensitive to touch because they have nerve endings wrapped around their roots. As soon as the hair is moved, nerve signals are sent to the brain, which means that you can feel the lightest touch of something even if it doesn't come into contact with your skin.

Skin color

As with eye color, the color of your skin depends on how much melanin it produces. The brown pigment protects the skin against the sun's harmful rays, so people native to hot countries tend to have darker skin. Fair skin has very little melanin in it and so it burns easily in the sun.

THIN SKIN

Your skin is at its thickest on the soles of your feet and at its thinnest on your eyelids, which is why you need darkness to get to sleep. See for yourself how that skin lets in light by closing your eyes in a lit room and waving your hands in front of them. Can you make out the moving shadows?

- *House dust mites love to gobble up your old skin cells! There are hundreds of thousands crawling around your house looking for lunch, but they're so small you can't see them.*

- *By the time you are an adult, you'll have around 5 million hairs all over your body. That's more hairs than a gorilla has! The only parts of your body where you have no hairs are your palms, soles and lips.*

- *Because your skin is busy renewing itself all the time, the old cells drop off all over the place. In fact, you just shed about 30,000 dead skin cells in the last minute!*

- *It takes about four weeks for your skin cells to get to the epidermis surface, die and drop off. That means you get a new skin every month!*

 # Touch

DID YOU KNOW?

- *You're sweating every minute of the day! You have more than two million sweat glands all over your body that are working all the time, but they work harder when you're hot.*

- *You have lots of sensors inside your body, too. These tell you about feelings such as a tummy ache or sore muscles.*

- *If you are right-handed, your left armpit will sweat more than your right. If you're left-handed, your right armpit will be the sweatier one!*

- *One of the substances secreted by other glands in your skin is naturally antibacterial. Without it, you would go moldy!*

What lies beneath

Underneath the epidermis is the dermis. This inner layer of skin is very much alive as it's where all those nerve endings are, along with blood vessels, sweat glands and hair follicles.

Super sensors

You have at least eight kinds of sensors in your skin of different shapes and sizes. They send signals to the brain about whether what you are touching is hot or cold, rough or smooth, wet or dry, hard or soft. These nerve endings can also detect levels of pressure, vibrations and pain. There are more than a thousand of them in just one square inch of skin!

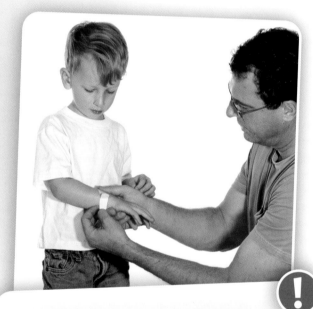

(!) OUCH!

You have more pain sensors in your skin than any other kind. Pain may not be pleasant, but it acts as a warning that your body is being damaged in some way. It makes you respond by either moving away from the pain source or taking care of the injury. Pain messages don't travel quite as quickly as touch signals, so if you bump into something, you feel the impact before the pain! This also explains why it sometimes helps to 'rub it better'.

Hot and cold

The sensors that respond to temperature are called thermoreceptors. If you hold something from the freezer, the coldness makes them shrink and this movement sends a message to the brain so it works out that what you are touching is cold. A rise in temperature makes these endings swell, so your brain receives messages that tell you something is hot. If it's really hot, your brain will quickly send messages to your muscles to pull your hand away!

Goose bumps

One of your body's responses to cold is goose bumps! These pimples are caused by muscles pulling on the hairs to make them stand on end to trap warm air next to the skin.

Nice and soft

As with our other senses, what we touch can affect our mood. Things like cuddling up in a soft blanket or stroking a furry pet can help us to relax.

Sensitivity

Some parts of your body have more feeling in them than others, depending on how many sensors they have. The parts of the body with the fewest sensors are the middle of your lower back and your outer thighs. Have a gentle poke around different areas of your back and you'll soon find the part that is the least sensitive!

👋 Looking with the lips

One very touch-sensitive area is the lips, as they have high numbers of touch sensors packed into a small space. This is why babies are always sticking things in their mouths – it's the best way for them to explore!

TOUCH TEST

See how much information you get from your sense of touch by doing the activities in the pocket on the inside of the cover!

👋 Feely fingertips

You normally feel things with your fingers, so the fingertips have a higher concentration of touch sensors than anywhere else in your body. Look closely at the ends of your fingers. The patterns of loops and whorls that you see are what make your fingerprints unique and are there to help you grip smooth objects.

👋 Reading by touch

People who are blind or have impaired vision can read and write using braille, a system of raised dots that are read by running the fingers over them. The system was invented by Frenchman Louis Braille, who was blinded as a young child after an accident in his father's workshop.

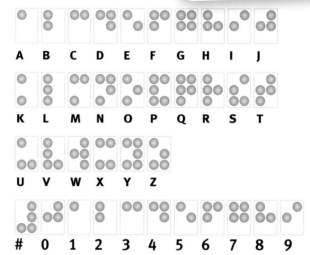

A B C D E F G H I J
K L M N O P Q R S T
U V W X Y Z
\# 0 1 2 3 4 5 6 7 8 9

👋 See for yourself

To have a good look at one of your fingerprints without using ink, find a pencil that is HB or softer and use it to color in a fingertip-sized section on a piece of white paper. Rub a fingertip on the grey area and then stick a piece of clear tape on the fingertip. Gently peel off the tape and stick it to another piece of white paper. Get a friend to do the same and see how your patterns compare!

DID YOU KNOW?

- There are no glands in the lips that produce the sweat and oily stuff (called sebum) that keep the rest of your skin soft. That's why they dry out so easily!

- There is no cure for cold sores. Once you've had one, you will get them on and off for the rest of your life!

- 1 in 500 people has an extra finger or toe! Baseball player Antonio Alfonseca has an extra finger on each of his hands and an extra toe on each of his feet.

- Soccer player Paulo Diogo lost the top half of his finger when he caught his wedding ring in a metal barrier during a goal celebration. The referee was not sympathetic – he gave him a yellow card for wasting time!

Touch

DID YOU KNOW?

- *Bee stings go deep into the skin and what cause pain and swelling are the toxins in the sting. It has been discovered that these chemicals can help conditions such as arthritis: bee venom therapy involves having the skin stung by lots of bees!*

- *Blood-sucking insects that you don't manage to scratch away will leave you with an itchy bite. What causes the itchiness is the skin's reaction to stuff in the insect's saliva.*

- *Only female mosquitoes want to feed on your blood! They need the protein in a tasty 'blood meal' to produce their eggs.*

- *The most painful sting on the planet comes from the bullet ant, causing agony that lasts a whole 24 hours. Lots of stings at the same time can even be fatal.*

Under pressure

The largest of your touch sensors are called Pacinian endings. They're a hundred times bigger than the smallest sensors, but they're still tiny (around a fiftieth of an inch or 0.5 mm). These endings look a bit like squashed onions and are there to make you feel pressure and vibrations. They're so sensitive that they can sense vibrations an inch away from your skin!

Taste and touch

The tongue has lots of touch sensors so that you can feel the texture of food and tell the difference between a cooked carrot and a raw one. They're sensitive enough to feel something as small as a hair in your mouth too!

What's that itch?

If you feel a light tickle on your skin, the brain's response is to make you scratch it. This reflex is to protect you from any bugs that might be trying to bite you or burrow into your skin! The only trouble is that this response is quite hard to control, so you can end up scratching itchy skin that is better left alone if it's due to something like eczema.

THAT TICKLES!

For most people, being tickled makes them laugh. No one knows why tickling is funny…or why it isn't, if you're not in the mood. It's also a mystery why it's difficult to tickle yourself!

Smart touch

The human sense of touch is so highly developed that we can carry out complex tasks by touch alone. A pianist, for example, can play a tune without looking at the keys. Try doing something like tying your shoelaces without looking at what your hands are doing. Can you manage it just by using touch?

Problems with skin

Skin usually heals very well: if you cut yourself, the blood clotting process begins within seconds until eventually a scabby shield is formed while the new skin grows underneath. Many skin problems, though, may need a little medical help.

Pimples

Glands in your dermis secrete an oily substance, sebum, through little holes in your skin called pores. If a pore gets blocked with too much sebum or dirt, dead skin cells and bacteria get trapped under the skin and a yellow-headed pimple appears. These glands work overtime during the teenage years so some teenagers get lots of pimples, known as acne.

LEAVE THOSE ZITS ALONE!

If a pimple appears on your skin, don't try to pop it! You can cause an infection that will look far worse than a pimple and you could leave yourself with a scar.

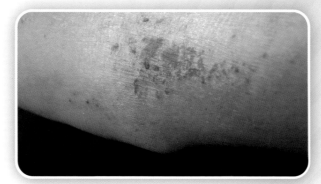

Eczema

Someone with eczema has sensitive skin cells that become easily irritated and form dry, itchy patches on the skin. Eczema is very common, especially in young children, and is often linked to allergies.

Fungal infections

Fungus is a harmless germ that is always sitting around on your skin without you noticing. Sometimes, though, the fungus can get out of control and make you itch! This is when the skin has a fungal infection, such as athlete's foot or ringworm. These problems are easy to cure with an anti-fungal cream from the doctor.

DID YOU KNOW?

Under ultraviolet light, fungal skin infections glow in the dark!

Skin growths

There are lots of viruses that can affect the skin cells and cause harmless skin growths, such as warts. These lumps and bumps will often clear up by themselves over time, but can be treated if they are painful or ugly to look at! Liquid nitrogen causes instant frostbite on healthy skin, but can be used to freeze away these abnormal skin cells.

DID YOU KNOW?

- *Maggots love to feast on dead flesh, so they have been used for thousands of years to help clean and heal wounds. The greedier ones eat the other maggots too!*

- *People in the Middle Ages used to 'cure' a wart by rubbing it with a piece of meat that they then buried. They believed that as the meat rotted in the ground, the wart disappeared too. Warts heal in time anyway, so they were wasting perfectly good bits of meat!*

- *The black dots in a wart are its blood supply.*

- *Skin can be grown in a laboratory! If someone has badly damaged skin, such as from a burn, a few of their healthy skin cells are taken. These cells multiply until a sheet is formed that can then be attached to the injured area in a skin graft operation.*

 # Touch

DID YOU KNOW?

- *The nastiest nettle plant is New Zealand's ongaonga tree. Its extra large stinging spines give you extra painful stings!*

- *Plants can give you a rash that is as sore as a bug's sting! Poison ivy is loaded with a clear, skin-irritating oil and just brushing against it is enough to give you itchy blisters, redness and swelling.*

- *You shouldn't take a bath after coming into contact with poison ivy, as the oil may spread through the water to other parts of the body. Shower it away instead!*

- *The sea nettle isn't a nettle, but it will give you a painful sting: it's a type of jellyfish.*

Taking care of the skin

Just because you get new skin every month, that doesn't mean you don't need to look after it! Your skin works hard to protect you and keep you warm, so return the favor and take good care of it.

Keep it clean

Your skin is the only organ that you need to wash! It needs to be clean to do its job properly, so using mild soap and water once a day will keep it smelling sweet and in good condition. Don't wash more often unless you really have to, as over washing can upset the skin's balance too and make it dry.

USING CREAMS

When you're young, your skin is usually moist enough without having to put anything extra on it. If for any reason you do have dry, flaky skin, use a cream that has no perfume or color in it.

Be safe in the sun

Your skin will darken when you go out into the sun, producing more melanin to help prevent burning. It can't do the job all by itself, though, so make sure you use a high-protection sunscreen (factor 30 or over) and wear a hat when you're having fun in the sun. Sunburn can be very painful and make you feel ill; it may also cause lasting damage to the skin cells, leading to wrinkles and skin cancer in later life.

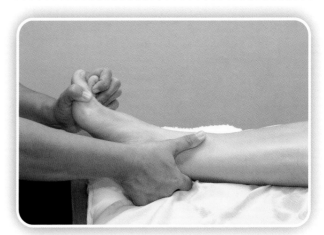

Marvelous massage

Athletes often have massages to help their muscles recover after a gruelling event. Even if you haven't just played any sport, having the skin and muscles massaged feels good and can even help you sleep. Try massaging your mum's hands and fingers with a little hand cream and see how relaxed she feels afterward!

 Super sensitive animals

Your sense of touch is very useful, but you don't rely on it as much as these creatures do!

Spider

A spider that spins webs has poor eyesight but is very sensitive to vibrations. An insect that flies into the web and gets trapped will struggle to free itself, sending vibrations along the silk threads to the spider. Sensing the movement, the spider will dash over to the insect and gobble it up!

Tiger

Like domestic cats, tigers have sensitive whiskers to help them get around in the dark and catch prey. Whiskers sense tiny amounts of movement because they are rooted deeply in the skin and have a capsule of blood around the base. When the hair moves, ripples in the blood amplify that movement and trigger nerve messages to the brain.

Octopus

An octopus has hundreds of touch-sensitive suckers on each of its eight arms, which it uses to feel around for prey, and is able to tell the difference between rough and smooth surfaces. Octopuses can do amazing things with their skin, too: they can change color to blend in with their background or ward off predators.

EXTRA ARMS

If for any reason an octopus loses one of its arms, it can just grow a new one! The lost arm wriggles around the ocean by itself for a while before it dies…

Mole

Animals that live in dark environments have a keen sense of touch, which they need to survive. Moles spend most of their time underground, so have no need to see. Some species, such as the desert-dwelling golden mole, have eyes that are covered with skin and fur – it looks like a golden hairball with legs!

DID YOU KNOW?

- *Camels don't feel the heat like we do. They begin to sweat only in temperatures higher than 106º F (41º C), saving over a gallon of water a day.*

- *Marine bloodworms have such thin skin that you can see their blood flowing through the vessels underneath it!*

- *Animals can have extra toes, too. Ginger tabby Jake has seven toes altogether on each paw, more than any other cat in the world!*

- *What make catfish look like cats are their barbels. These look like whiskers and have the same function, helping the fish to seek out prey by touch in murky waters.*

Test your knowledge!

 **Sight**

Your sense of sight sent the words in this book to your brain, but how many of them stayed there? See how much you've leared by answering these questions on all your senses without peeking at the answers on page 47. If you really can't remember an answer, see if you can find it in the book first!

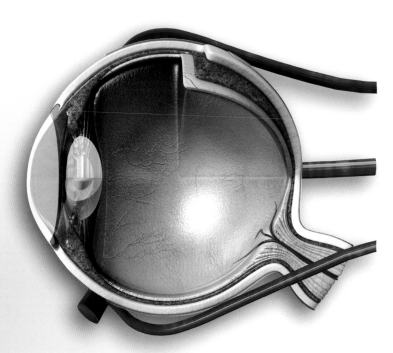

1. What is the light-sensitive lining at the back of the eye called?

a) The iris.
b) The retina.
c) The cornea.

2. Which of your glands make tears?

a) Sebaceous glands.
b) Sweat glands.
c) Lacrimal glands.

3. What is the name of the brown pigment that gives your eyes, hair and skin their color?

a) Lanolin.
b) Melanin.
c) Melatonin.

4. When you go into a dark room, what do your pupils do?

a) Nothing.
b) They get smaller.
c) They get bigger.

5. What is the only part of your body that has no blood supply?

a) The cornea.
b) The eyelid.
c) The sclera.

6. What are the cells called that let you see colors?

a) Blood cells.
b) Rods.
c) Cones.

7. Cataracts affect which part of the eye?

a) The iris.
b) The lens.
c) The optic nerve.

8. Laser eye surgery can be used to correct bad eyesight. What part of the eye does it alter?

a) The cornea.
b) The eyebrow.
c) The sclera.

9. Which animal has the largest eyes on the planet?

a) The giant squid.
b) The African elephant.
c) The giraffe.

10. Which of these creatures has compound eyes?

a) A dog.
b) A bee.
c) A woodpecker.

Smell

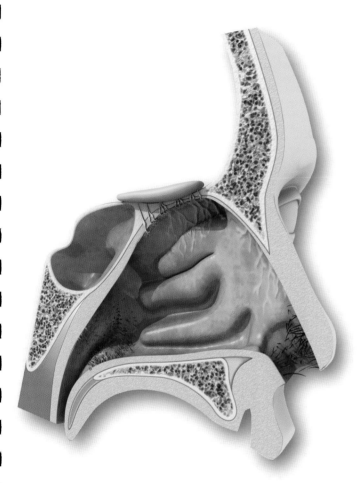

1. What is the name of the hollow space behind your nose?

a) The olfactory bulb.
b) The nasal cavity.
c) The palate.

2. Your sense of smell is how many times more sensitive than your sense of taste?

a) 100.
b) 1,000.
c) 10,000.

3. What does fresh sweat smell of?

a) Nothing.
b) Oranges.
c) Body odor.

4. What happens to all the muscles in your body when you sneeze?

a) Nothing.
b) They relax.
c) They contract.

5. Animals use special smells to send messages to each other. What are these smells called?

a) Homophones.
b) Pheromones.
c) Microphones.

 # Taste

1. Where on your tongue are the largest papillae?

a) The center.
b) The back.
c) The tip.

2. How many taste buds do you have on your tongue?

a) About 100.
b) About 1,000.
c) About 10,000.

3. How many basic tastes are there?

a) 2.
b) 5.
c) 8.

4. What happens to your taste buds if they are cold?

a) They don't work as well.
b) They work the same.
c) They work better.

5. Which animal has the biggest tongue on the planet?

a) The blue whale.
b) The brown bear.
c) The hippopotamus.

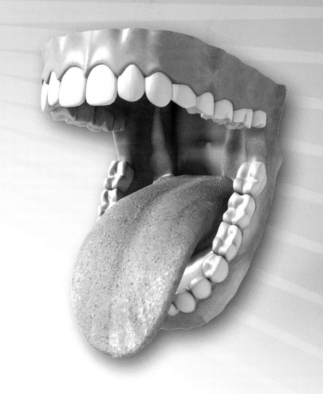

Hearing

1. How many main sections does each of your ears have?

a) 1.
b) 3.
c) 7.

2. The smallest bone in your body is in your ear. What is its name?

a) The stirrup.
b) The eardrum.
c) The cochlea.

3. Which section of your ear is filled with fluid?

a) The outer ear.
b) The middle ear.
c) The inner ear.

4. Your eardrum is made of what?

a) Skin.
b) Bone.
c) Jelly.

5. What is sound measured in?

a) Decimals.
b) Decibels.
c) Decagons.

6. What is the loudest creature on Earth?

a) The chimpanzee.
b) The lion.
c) The blue whale.

7. What should you use to clean inside your ear?

a) A cotton swab.
b) Nothing.
c) A finger.

8. What is the name for a constant noise inside one or both ears?

a) Tetanus.
b) Tinnitus.
c) Typhus.

9. Which part of your ear helps you to keep your balance?

a) The outer ear.
b) The middle ear.
c) The inner ear.

10. The African elephant has larger ears than any other animal. Apart from hearing, what does it use them for?

a) To cool down.
b) To carry things.
c) To keep warm.

Touch

1. What is the name of the layer of skin that you can see?

a) The dermis.
b) The follicle.
c) The epidermis.

2. How many hairs cover your body?

a) About 5,000.
b) About 50,000.
c) About 5,000,000.

3. On which part of your body is the skin thinnest?

a) The hands.
b) The eyelids.
c) The feet.

4. You have several different types of sensor in your skin. Which do you have the most of?

a) Pain sensors.
b) Pressure sensors.
c) Heat sensors.

5. Which part of your body has the most touch sensors?

a) The back.
b) The fingertips.
c) The forehead.

6. What are your largest touch sensors called?

a) Pacific endings.
b) Peruvian endings.
c) Pacinian endings.

7. What makes a wart appear on your skin?

a) A virus.
b) An insect bite.
c) A fungus.

8. A sea nettle can give you a nasty sting, but what is it?

a) Seaweed.
b) A jellyfish.
c) Coral.

9. What is the lowest protection factor you should use on your skin when out in the sun?

a) Factor 5.
b) Factor 10.
c) Factor 30.

10. What does a spider sense when it has caught something in its web?

a) Vibrations.
b) Sound.
c) Heat.

ANSWERS: